SHORT WALKS
MADE EASY

NEW FOREST

Ordnance Survey

Contents

Getting outside in the New Forest		6
We smile more when we're outside		8
Respecting the countryside		10
Using this guide		11
Walk 1	Fritham	**14**
Walk 2	Minstead	**20**
Photos	Scenes from the walks	26
Walk 3	Lyndhurst	**28**
Walk 4	Burley	**34**
Photos	Wildlife interest	40
Walk 5	Brockenhurst	**42**
Walk 6	Boldre	**48**
Walk 7	Beaulieu to Buckler's Hard	**54**
Photos	Cafés and pubs	60
Walk 8	Lepe	**62**
Walk 9	Sway	**68**
Walk 10	Keyhaven	**74**
Credits		80

Map symbols	Front cover flap
Accessibility and what to take	Back cover flap
Walk locations	Inside front cover
Your next adventure?	Inside back cover

2 Short Walks Made Easy

Walk 1
FRITHAM

Distance
4.7 miles / 7.6km

Time
2½ hours

Start/Finish
Fritham

Parking SO43 7HL
Forestry England car park, Fritham

Cafés/pubs
Royal Oak, Fritham

Delightful accessible walk for all, ending at a characterful old pub

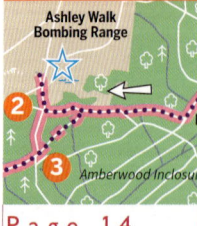

Page 14

Walk 2
MINSTEAD

Distance
4.7 miles / 7.5 km

Time
2½ hours

Start/Finish
Minstead

Parking SO43 7FY
Parking area off the green, Minstead

Cafés/pubs
Trusty Servant Inn; two tearooms

Picturesque village; award-winning garden; welcoming tearooms

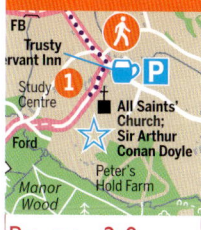

Page 20

Walk 3
LYNDHURST

Distance
5 miles / 8 km

Time
2½ hours   CATCH A BUS

Start/Finish
Lyndhurst

Parking SO43 7DA
Forestry England Bolton's Bench car park

Cafés/pubs
Lyndhurst; Crown Stirrup

Ridge-top heath, ancient bluebell woods and Balanos the Dragon

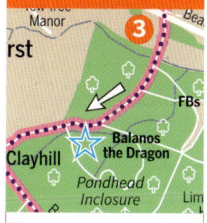

Page 28

Walk 4
BURLEY

Distance
4.25 miles / 6.8 km

Time
2¼ hours   CATCH A BUS

Start/Finish
Burley

Parking BH24 4AB
Burley car park

Cafés/pubs
Burley

Witchcraft; a smuggler's hoard; New Forest Cider; Castle Hill views

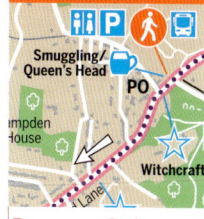

Page 34

Contents 3

Walk 5

BROCKENHURST

Distance
4.3 miles/7km

Time
2¼ hours

Start/Finish
Brockenhurst

Parking SO42 7TW
Brockenhurst Station car park

Cafés/pubs
Brockenhurst

The Watersplash; a snake catcher legend; a lovely heathland plain

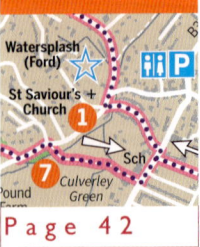

Page 42

Walk 6

BOLDRE

Distance
3.9 miles/6.25km

Time
2 hours

Start/Finish
Church of St John the Baptist, Boldre

Parking SO41 5PG
Church car park

Cafés/pubs
Red Lion, Boldre

Hilltop church with fascinating history; fine wooded nature reserve

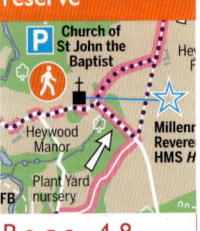

Page 48

Walk 7

BEAULIEU TO BUCKLER'S HARD

Distance
4.8 miles/7.7km

Time
2½ hours

Start/Finish
Beaulieu

Parking SO42 7PJ
Beaulieu car park

Cafés/pubs
Beaulieu; Buckler's Hard

Beaulieu and its scenic river; the Solent Way to historic Buckler's Hard

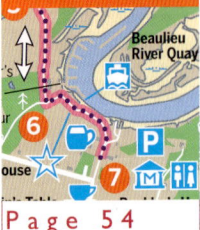

Page 54

Walk 8

LEPE

Distance
4.5 miles/7.25km

Time
2½ hours

Start/Finish
Lepe Country Park

Parking SO45 1AD
Lepe Country Park car park

Cafés/pubs
The Lookout, Lepe Country Park

Rich D-Day history; café with fabulous Solent and Isle of Wight views

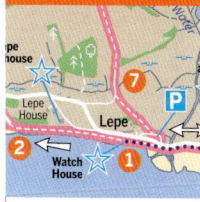

Page 62

Walk 9

SWAY

Distance
4 miles/6.5km

Time
2 hours

Start/Finish
Sway

Parking SO41 6BA
Sway Railway Station car park

Cafés/pubs
Sway

Lovely mixed woodland; Hincheslea Bog views; heather-covered heath

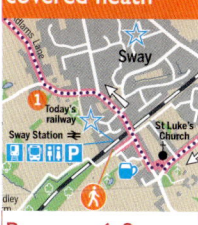

Page 68

Walk 10

KEYHAVEN

Distance
5.1 miles/8.2km

Time
2½ hours

Start/Finish
Keyhaven

Parking SO41 0TP
Keyhaven car park

Cafés/pubs
The Gun Inn; Chequers Inn; Hurst Castle café

Salt production history; top birdwatching site; ferry to Hurst Castle

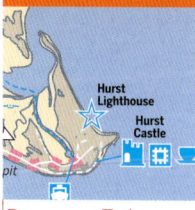

Page 74

Contents 5

GETTING OUTSIDE IN THE NEW FOREST

> " you can see ponies, donkeys, cattle, pigs and sheep roaming freely

OS Champion
Sue Barrett

Lepe foreshore

A very warm welcome to the new Short Walks Made Easy guide to the New Forest – what a fantastic selection of leisurely walks we have for you!

The New Forest National Park was created in 2006. It covers an area of 220 square miles, almost wholly within Hampshire, with 26 miles of coastline. It has a wonderful mix of habitats including ancient woodland, heathland, valley mires, grassland, salt marsh and rivers. These habitats support over 20,000 species of animals, plants and fungi and the New Forest is nationally and internationally recognised as an important conservation designation. These walks allow you to explore the New Forest's natural beauty and wildlife and appreciate its tranquillity. You can spot wading birds, geese and ducks around Keyhaven, and in Brockenhurst you can find an ancient yew tree.

Created as a royal hunting ground in 1079, there is also a rich cultural heritage to discover. The ancient rights given to the New Forest Commoners allow them to graze their livestock and so you can see ponies, donkeys, cattle, pigs and sheep roaming freely.

There are stories of smuggling to uncover in Burley; 18th-century shipbuilding to delve into at Buckler's Hard; and you can learn of the strategic importance of the area in both World Wars at Lyndhurst Heritage Centre, Lepe and Beaulieu.

These walks take you to many delightful villages such as Fritham, Minstead and Boldre, where their characterful pubs add even more historical interest.

Sue Barrett,
OS Champion

WE SMILE MORE WHEN WE'RE OUTSIDE

Culverley Green, near Brockenhurst

Whether it's a short walk during our lunch break or a full day's outdoor adventure, we know that a good dose of fresh air is just the tonic we all need.

At Ordnance Survey (OS), we're passionate about helping more people to get outside more often. It sits at the heart of everything we do, and through our products and services, we aim to help you lead an active outdoor lifestyle, so that you can live longer, stay younger and enjoy life more.

We firmly believe the outdoors is for everyone, and we want to help you find the very best Great Britain has to offer. We are blessed with an island that is beautiful and unique, with a rich and varied landscape. There are coastal paths to meander along, woodlands to explore, countryside to roam, and cities to uncover. Our trusted source of inspirational content is bursting with ideas for places to go, things to do and easy beginner's guides on how to get started.

It can be daunting when you're new to something, so we want to bring you the know-how from the people who live and breathe the outdoors. To help guide us, our team of awe-inspiring OS Champions share their favourite places to visit, hints and tips for outdoor adventures, as well as tried and tested accessible, family- and wheelchair-friendly routes. We hope that you will feel inspired to spend more time outside and reap the physical and mental health benefits that the outdoors has to offer. With our handy guides, paper and digital mapping, and exciting new apps, we can be with you every step of the way.

To find out more visit os.uk/getoutside

RESPECTING
THE COUNTRYSIDE

You can't beat getting outside in the British countryside, but it's vital that we leave no trace when we're enjoying the great outdoors.

Let's make sure that generations to come can enjoy the countryside just as we do.

 Leave no trace

 Keep dogs under control; bin and bag waste

 Do not light fires; only BBQ at official sites

 Leave gates as you find them

 Keep to footpaths and open access land

 Plan ahead for your trip

For more details please visit gov.uk/countryside-code

USING THIS GUIDE

Easy-to-follow New Forest walks for all

Before setting off

Check the walk information panel to plan your outing

- Consider using **Public transport** where flagged. If driving, note the satnav postcode for the car park under **Parking**
- The suggested **Time** is based on a gentle pace
- Note the availability of **Cafés**, tearooms and pubs, and **Toilets**

Terrain and hilliness

- **Terrain** indicates the nature of the route surface
- Any rises and falls are noted under **Hilliness**

Walking with your dog?

- This panel states where **Dogs** must be on a lead and how many stiles there are – in case you need to lift your dog
- Keep dogs on leads where there are livestock and between April and August in forest and on grassland where there are ground-nesting birds

A perfectly pocket-sized walking guide

- Handily sized for ease of use on each walk
- When not being read, it fits nicely into a pocket...
- ...so between points, put this book in the pocket of your coat, trousers or day sack and enjoy your stroll in glorious countryside – we've made it pocket-sized for a reason!

Flexibility of route presentation to suit all readers

- **Not comfortable map reading?** Then use the simple-to-follow route profile and accompanying route description and pictures
- **Happy to map read?** New-look walk mapping makes it easier for you to focus on the route and the points of interest along the way
- **Read the insightful Did you know?, Local legend, Stories behind the walk** and **Nature notes** to help you make the most of your day out and to enjoy all that each walk has to offer

OS information about the walk

- Many of the features and symbols shown are taken from Ordnance Survey's celebrated **Explorer** mapping, designed to help people across Great Britain enjoy leisure time spent outside

- National Grid reference for the start point
- Explorer sheet map covering the route

OS information
🚶 SU 231141
Explorer OL22

The easy-to-use walk map

- **Large-scale** mapping for ultra-clear route finding

- **Numbered points** at key turns along the route that tie in with the route instructions and respective points marked on the profile

- **Pictorial symbols** for intuitive map reading, see Map Symbols on the front cover flap

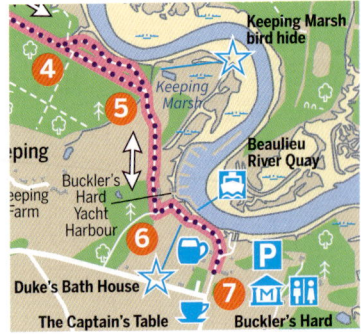

The simple-to-follow walk profile

- Progress easily along the route using the illustrative profile, it has **numbered points** for key turning points and **graduated distance** markers

- Easy-read **route directions** with turn-by-turn detail

- Reassuring **route photographs** for each numbered point

5 ► Go through the gate and along a boardwalk to visit Keeping Marsh bird hide.

Using QR codes

- Scan each QR code to see the route in Ordnance Survey's OS Maps App
NB You may need to download a scanning app if you have an older phone

- OS Maps will open the route automatically if you have it installed. If not, the route will open in the web version of OS Maps

- Please click **Start Route** button to begin navigating or **Download Route** to store the route for offline use

New Forest

WALK 1

FRITHAM

Peacefully situated in the northern half of the New Forest, the village of Fritham is a popular spot thanks to its attractive location and its pub, the 17th-century Royal Oak, a charming thatched hostelry, full of character. Although quiet today, albeit well frequented by visitors, Fritham was once the location of a gunpowder factory, while during World War II a bombing range was established nearby. This walk takes in both woodland and heathland with some good views.

OS information	
SU 231141 Explorer OL22	
Distance	4.7 miles/7.6km
Time	2½ hours
Start/Finish	Fritham
Parking SO43 7HL	Forestry England car park, Fritham (just beyond pub)
Public toilets	None
Cafés/pubs	Royal Oak, Fritham
Terrain	Gravel tracks and grassy paths
Hilliness	Gently undulating
Footwear	Winter 🥾 Spring/Summer/Autumn 👟

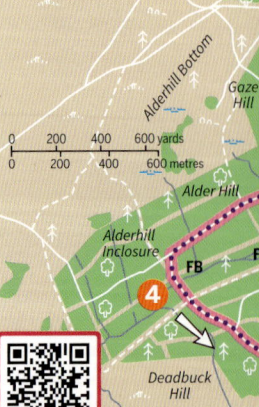

14 Short Walks Made Easy

Public transport
Very infrequent bus service – just one a day on Tuesdays and Fridays: hants.gov.uk/transport

Accessibility

Suitable throughout for powered wheelchairs and all-terrain pushchairs using shortcut to

Dogs
Welcome but beware cyclists on multi-use forest tracks. No stiles

Did you know? On this walk and on others in this guide you will pass numbered posts at the trackside, which are used along the cycle network established by Foresty England across the New Forest. These gravel tracks provide a good all-weather surface for walkers too. You can download a cycle map from the National Park or Forestry England websites or buy maps locally that show the numbers of the wooden waymarker posts, so you can locate where you are when you come across one.

Much of this route goes through what are known as 'inclosures': timber plantations managed by Forestry England. Much of the planting is fast-growing conifers, such as Douglas fir, that are grown for their timber.

Local legend Dating back to the 17th century, the Royal Oak is one of the oldest pubs in the New Forest. Its founding predates local written records.

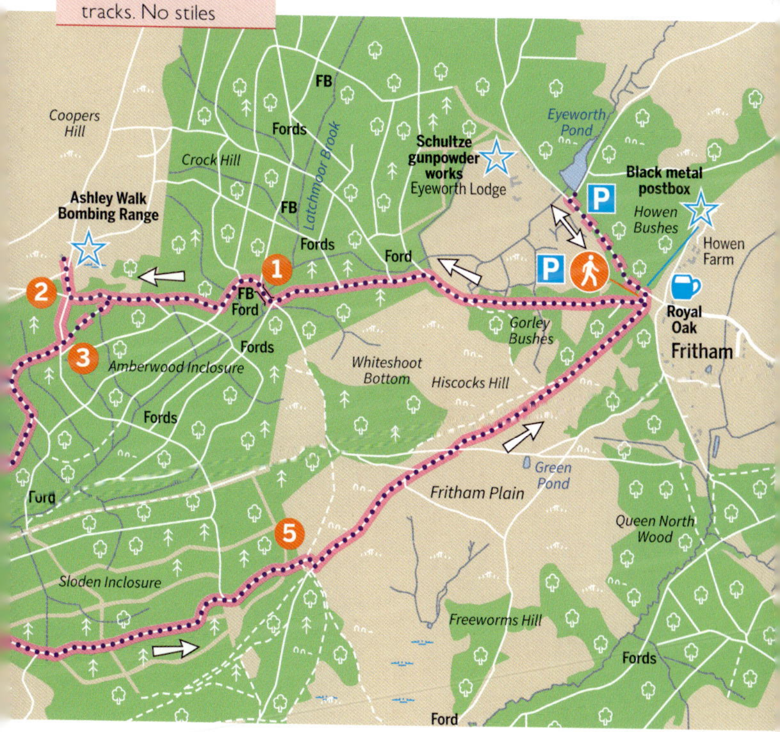

Walk 1 Fritham

STORIES BEHIND THE WALK

☆ **Schultze gunpowder works** From the 1860s to the 1920s Fritham was home to the Schultze Gunpowder Factory, which manufactured smokeless gunpowder, used in sporting guns. Man-made Eyeworth Pond, one of the New Forest's beauty spots, was created by damming a brook to provide water for the factory, based at Eyeworth Lodge. The pond is just a 10-minute walk down the quiet no-through road from the car park – there is a car park there too.

☆ **Black metal postbox** Little evidence remains of the former gunpowder works, a thriving industry in its time and a major employer in the New Forest. However, at the entrance to the car park there is a black postbox, which was erected to make the postman's life easier before motor vehicles, saving him the journey down to the factory and back up again.

Black metal post-box ☆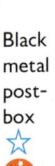

🅿️ Forestry England Fritham car park — Gorley Bushes — ½ mile — 1 mile — Bridge (Latchmore Brook) ❶ — Post 11

- ▶ With your back to the road and car park entrance, take the **right-hand** fork past a barrier, signed Cycle route to Frogham only, post 14 next to it.
- ▶ Continue along the gravel track, passing posts 13 and 12, to reach a footbridge.

❶ ▶ Cross the bridge and fork **left** at post 11 just after it.
▶ Keep **straight on** at post 10, past a gated track that forks left (a shortcut to ❸), heading uphill to a crossways at post 9, where the track levels.

16 Short Walks Made Easy

☆ Ashley Walk Bombing Range

During World War II the establishment of the bombing range – passed on this walk – shattered the peace of the area. A vast area of heathland – over 5,000 acres (equivalent to 2,833 football pitches) – was used to test a huge variety of explosives. By the end of the war the land was pockmarked with craters and defaced with rubble and targets, most removed thereafter. The small brick observation shelter near ❷ is the only surviving building.

☆ Ashley Walk Bombing Range (right)

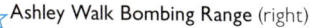

❷ ➡ The route turns left through the gate, but first, detour **right** and soon fork **left** across grass to Ashley Walk Bombing Range observation shelter (see above).

➡ Retrace your steps and go through the gate, down a grassy path through trees to a gravel track in 200 yards.

❸ ➡ Turn **right**. Ignoring side turnings continue on the meandering track for ¾ mile and then, after a straight section, curve **left** down to a footbridge. Before it, look out for the carved memorial bench (right) to naturalist and film-maker Eric Ashby.

Walk 1 Fritham

NATURE NOTES

The green at Fritham is rarely without ponies or donkeys.

The New Forest is one of the most significant areas for fungi in Britain, with about 2,700 species. Enjoy looking for them in autumn, but do not pick them.

The porcelain fungus grows on the trunks and fallen branches of dead beech trees. It lives up to its name as it has a shiny white appearance.

One of the more common species of fungi, the shaggy inkcap is a bell-shaped toadstool with a rough or shaggy surface. Due to its distinctive appearance it is also known as lawyer's wig.

Oyster mushrooms can be found at any season of the year. This fungus grows horizontally out of the dead or dying wood of deciduous trees.

If you have time, do turn left along the lane out of the car park and stroll the 500 yards to Eyeworth Pond. Created in the 19th century, it is a lovely spot to sit and relax, with water lilies and ducks to enjoy — you may spot a mandarin duck with its exotic plumage.

New Forest donkeys, mare and foal, at Fritham

Bridge (Latchmore Brook) — 2½ miles
3 miles
3½ miles

Sloden Inclosure

4 ▪ **Cross** the bridge and go through two gates, one after another.
▪ Keep **straight ahead** past a left turning and keep **ahead** again at a right turn. The track heads steadily uphill to a gate, where you leave the woodland.

5 ▪ Go through the gate and soon after bear **left** where another track joins from the right.
▪ Follow the level track across Fritham Plain back to the car park.

18 Short Walks Made Easy

Above: Eyeworth Pond water lillies
Below: porcelain fungus (left), oyster fungus (right)

Top: North American red oak leaves
Above: mandarin duck

Eyeworth Pond (500 yards, left)
Royal Oak (right)

Fritham Plain   Gorley Bushes

⑤ Gate   4 miles   4½ miles   **Black metal postbox**

Forestry England Fritham car park

☕ Royal Oak

Recommended by the *Good Pub Guide*, the award-winning pub, which has been run by the same family for over two decades, serves real ales straight from the cask and locally sourced ploughman's lunches. A pop-up shop selling New Forest farm produce is located in the pub garden. The meat comes from the family's own farm, adjoining the pub. Accommodation is available in hand-built shepherd's huts next door, with New Forest ponies a common sight on the green outside.

Walk 1 Fritham

WALK 2

MINSTEAD

The picturesque and unspoilt village of Minstead is situated a couple of miles north-west of Lyndhurst, not far from the A31. There's an attractive green, complete with replica stocks, an unusual church, where Sir Arthur Conan Doyle's grave can be found, a volunteer-run community shop and a welcoming pub, the Trusty Servant Inn. This walk follows quiet lanes, paths and forest tracks, passing lovely Chelsea gold medal-winning Furzey Gardens near the end, which are well worth a visit.

OS information

SU 281110
Explorer OL22

Distance
4.7 miles/7.5km

Time
2½ hours

Start/Finish
Minstead

Parking SO43 7FY
Parking area on the far side of the green from the pub, opposite Congleton Close; alternatively, by the church at the top end of Church Lane

Public toilets
None

Cafés/pubs
Trusty Servant Inn, Minstead; Acres Down Farm Cream Teas (seasonal); Furzey Gardens tearoom

Terrain
Quiet country lanes; field and woodland paths; gravel forest tracks

Hilliness
Gently undulating, with one moderate climb after ④

Footwear
Winter 🥾
Spring/Summer/Autumn 👟

Public transport

Very infrequent bus service – just one a day on Tuesdays and Fridays: hants.gov.uk/transport

Accessibility

Lane from 🚶 to ①; and between Rufus Stone, ⑦ and 🚶.

Dogs

Welcome but beware cyclists on multi-use forest tracks. Several stiles on the field path sections

Did you know? North of Furzey Gardens on the other side of the A31 is the Rufus Stone, a much-visited New Forest site, supposedly the location at which William II, known as William Rufus, was killed. William II, the third son of William the Conqueror, who claimed the area as a royal hunting forest (it was recorded as Nova Foresta in the Domesday survey of 1086), was referred to as William Rufus because of his red hair and ruddy complexion. The fateful arrow that killed him on 2 August 1100 was shot by nobleman Sir Walter Tyrrell. It was allegedly an accident but, because Rufus was an unpopular monarch, there was speculation.

If you want to extend the walk to visit the Rufus Stone – in fact a three-sided iron pillar which replaced an earlier stone – an out-and-back detour (crossing the A31 via an underpass) adds 1.8 miles/2.9km to the total route distance. There is a car park there though, if you'd rather drive.

Walk 2 Minstead

STORIES BEHIND THE WALK

All Saints' Church The oldest parts of the church, the nave and chancel, date from the 13th century, while the red brick construction is 18th-century or later. Of note inside is the three-tiered pulpit: the top level used for preaching, the middle for Bible readings and the lowest for the clerk to say 'Amens' after prayers. There are also two galleries and, to the north of the sanctuary, a small parlour-like private pew with its own fireplace, built for the inhabitants of Castle Malwood, a large house not far away.

Trusty Servant Inn The curious pub sign that depicts the 'trusty servant' shows a man with a pig's snout, a padlocked jaw to illustrate discretion, a donkey's ears, and a stag's feet to indicate his swiftness in running errands. The original 16th-century picture is at Winchester College. The 16th-century saying below the picture is thought to originate from the time when pupils at the college had their own personal servants.

- Trusty Servant Inn
- All Saints' Church
- Sir Arthur Conan Doyle

Parking area on opposite side of green

➤ Begin in Church Lane, with the Trusty Servant Inn on your right, and walk up to the church.

① ➤ Take the footpath along the **right-hand** side of the churchyard, leading down to a gravel drive. Turn **right** to the road and then go **left** along it.
➤ Continue on Newtown Road for ½ mile, ignoring turnings and keeping **ahead** past a phone box to reach a crossroads.

② Crossroads — 1 mile — Acres Down Cream Teas

22 Short Walks Made Easy

🌸 Furzey Gardens

Run as a social enterprise supporting people with learning difficulties, Furzey Gardens is a lovely place to visit (entrance to gardens by donation; gift shop and tearoom free to enter). There are 10 acres of delightful woodland gardens to explore with something for every season. In spring, the gardens' renowned collection of rhododendrons and azaleas are a blaze of colour. For children there are secret fairy doors to discover. There is also a 16th-century thatched cottage to look around (minsteadtrust.org.uk).

☆ Sir Arthur Conan Doyle

The grave of Doyle, who created Sherlock Holmes, is to be found at the rear of the church near its southern edge by an oak tree. He was originally buried in the garden of his home in Crowborough, Sussex, but was later reinterred here. He had a holiday home in the Minstead area which he used as his country retreat.

Forestry England Acres Down car park

Hart Hill
2 miles

1½ miles

W i c k   W o o d

2 ▶ Go **straight across** and down the no-through road to Acres Down Farm, crossing a footbridge and passing the tearoom (left).
▶ Continue along the lane round a right-hand bend to reach Forestry England's Acres Down car park.

3 ▶ Keep **ahead** past the barrier along a gravel cycle track (car park left).
▶ Take the first turning on the **right**, opposite post 97, dropping into a valley and then rising to a fork in the track.

NATURE NOTES

Minstead is surrounded by fenced pasture, used for grazing cattle and sheep. On the unenclosed New Forest land, ponies are the most common stock animals, numbering around 5,000, but you are also likely to encounter cattle, sheep, donkeys and pigs.

Native to Britain and found in the New Forest on heathland and in woodland, the fly agaric is a very distinctive and highly toxic fungus. It has a bright scarlet cap with white spots, and in literature is most often associated with fairy tales.

The laneside hedgerows around Minstead are a favourite habitat of whitethroats, rather shy summer visitors from Africa, with eponymous white throat and pale blue-grey head; and chaffinches, which are present year round. Male chaffinches are particularly colourful, with their pinkish-buff fronts.

In summer, look out for verge and hedgerow butterflies such as gatekeeper, ringlet and red admiral.

Furzey Gardens were first planted in 1922 and now contain a wide collection of rare and beautiful plants from around the world. *Nyssa sylvatica*, 'Sheffield Park', is renowned for its autumn colour at Furzey.

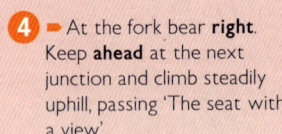

4 ▶ At the fork bear **right**. Keep **ahead** at the next junction and climb steadily uphill, passing 'The seat with a view'.

▶ Continue **ahead** on a grassy way over the level hilltop, keeping **ahead (right)** at all subsequent forks, soon sweeping round a broad right-hand bend and reaching a road (left).

5 ▶ **Cross** the road and turn **right** along the verge for 50 yards, forking **left** along a gravel track (fingerpost).

▶ Keep **left** at a fork after King's Garn then follow the gravel track to a lane corner in 400 yards.

Asters, Furzey Gardens

Top: donkeys
Middle: fly agaric
Bottom: red admiral

Furzey Gardens

3½ miles — 4 miles — 4½ miles — Trusty Servant Inn

Parking area on opposite side of green

6 ▶ Turn immediately **left** across a stile.
▶ In 400 yards, go over another stile and turn **right**, descending to cross a footbridge. Soon after, pass through a kissing-gate on the **right** to reach Furzey Gardens car park.

7 ▶ Carry on down to the road junction.
▶ Turn **right** along the lane then **right** again. Take the first footpath on the **left**, which leads to another road. Turn **right** back to the start.

Walk 2 Minstead

This page (clockwise): Hurst Castle, from the Isle of Wight; Beaulieu River estuary, Lepe; donkeys at Beaulieu; pasture near Minstead
Opposite (clockwise): the former wheelwright's workshop, Perkins' Piece, Boldre; Millennium Window, St John the Baptist Church, Boldre; Beaulieu River Millennium Beacon

WALK 3

LYNDHURST

Known as the capital of the New Forest, Lyndhurst is the largest village in the national park. The New Forest Heritage Centre, which houses a museum, gift shop and café, is well worth a visit (free entry). In the village churchyard you'll find the grave of former Lyndhurst resident, Alice Hargreaves, née Liddell, the inspiration for Lewis Carroll's *Alice in Wonderland*. This walk explores the lovely open heath and beautiful woodland on the east side of Lyndhurst.

OS information
SU 303081
Explorer OL22

Distance
5 miles/8km

Time
2½ hours

Start/Finish
Lyndhurst

Parking SO43 7DA
Forestry England Bolton's Bench car park

Public toilets
Lyndhurst – adjacent to the New Forest Heritage Centre

Cafés/pubs
Lyndhurst; Crown Stirrup pub, 250 yards from ❹

Terrain
Heath and woodland tracks

Hilliness
Gently undulating

Footwear
Winter 🥾
Spring/Summer/Autumn 👟

Public transport
Bluestar bus service 6 between Southampton and Lymington stops outside the Fire Station, opposite ➊: bluestarbus.co.uk

Accessibility
Suitable throughout for powered wheelchairs and all-terrain pushchairs

Dogs
Welcome but beware cyclists on multi-use forest tracks. No stiles

Did you know? Commoners are people who own or rent land in the New Forest and they benefit from common rights, of which there are six. Pasture, the most important right still in use today, allows animals such as ponies, cattle and donkeys to graze on the open forest. Another right still in use is mast or pannage, which allows pigs to graze on acorns and beech mast (nuts). Other rights include collecting wood (known as estovers) and peat for fuel (turbary).

Local legend The only dragon currently present in the New Forest (the work of wood carver Perry Bond) can be found in Pondhead Inclosure on this walk. Legend has it that Bolton's Bench mound was formed by the corpse of a slain dragon (see Walk 4), the victorious knight dying on top of it; a yew tree then grew from his yew-wood bow.

Walk 3 Lyndhurst 29

STORIES BEHIND THE WALK

● **Alice's grave** The Victorian Church of St Michael and All Angels, with its strikingly tall spire, stands on raised ground overlooking the village. Built in red brick, it contains stained glass by Edward Burne-Jones and a fresco by Lord Leighton. But it is best known for the grave (found round the back of the church) of former Lyndhurst resident, Alice Hargreaves, née Liddell, who was the inspiration for Lewis Carroll's *Alice in Wonderland*. She met the author as a little girl, and later married Reginald Hargreaves.

☆ **Bolton's Bench** The car park where the walk starts takes its name from a distinctive landmark. The yew trees atop the nearby knoll were planted as a memorial to the Duke of Bolton, who was the New Forest Master Keeper in the 18th century. They are now surrounded by benches. It's worth walking to the top for the views.

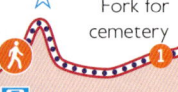

Bolton's Bench ☆ — Fork for cemetery ① — ② Trig point — ③ B3056, Beaulieu Road — Balanos the Dragon ☆

½ mile — 1 mile

Lyndhurst bus stop

Pondhead Inclosure

P Forestry England Bolton's Bench car park

➤ From the car park, head **left**, towards the war memorial, along the access drive.

➤ Detour **right** to the top of Bolton's Bench hillock then return to the drive.

➤ Bear **right** and continue to a fork.

① ➤ Where the drive forks left to the cemetery, keep **ahead** along a gravel track (thatched cricket pavilion, right).

➤ Go past a barrier, soon bearing **right** across grass to a trig point and bench.

② ➤ Continue over the grass parallel to the road for another 200 yards.

➤ Turn **right** down a gravel track to another barrier and meet the road.

New Forest Heritage Centre

There's a museum, exhibition gallery and reference library, as well as a gift shop and café at the New Forest Heritage Centre, which is a must for all visitors. It is wheelchair accessible and well-behaved dogs are welcome. Here you can learn all about the history of the New Forest and its traditions, the different habitats and variety of wildlife, and conservation work. It's also family friendly with interactive activities, quizzes and colouring sheets (newforestheritage.org.uk).

☆ King's House

Situated at the west end of Lyndhurst High Street, this handsome 17th-century building is the traditional seat of Crown authority in the New Forest. Formerly known as the Queen's House, it changed its name after the death of the late Queen in keeping with the custom of adopting the title of the monarch of the day. It is the local headquarters of Forestry England, which manages Crown lands in the Forest. It is also home to the Court of Verderers, which oversees the rights of commoners (see page 29).

4 Crown Stirrup (ahead, 250 yards)

1½ miles · 2 miles · Park Hill · Beechen Lane

3 ➤ **Cross** the road and continue along the gravel track opposite. Soon go through a gate between houses into Pondhead Inclosure.
➤ Cross a bridge and keep ahead at all junctions. Look out for Williams Copse plaque on the right and beyond it a path on the left into a clearing to see Balanos the dragon (pictured below).
➤ Further on the track runs along the boundary of the inclosure to reach a gate and small parking area just beyond.

NATURE NOTES

There's every chance you'll see New Forest ponies along The Ridge track (from ⑥ onwards). The ponies have been called the architects of the Forest landscape – without their grazing and that of the cattle and deer, the New Forest would become overgrown with brambles and gorse.

During the autumn round-up of the ponies (called the drift), when they are checked over, their tails are cut by agisters (employees of the verderers) to show that the pony has been paid for. Each agister has their own mark, and this signifies the agister's area in which the owner of the pony lives.

Pondhead Inclosure

④ ► To visit the Crown Stirrup pub, cross the car park, go through the gate **ahead** and along the path for 250 yards.
► Otherwise, turn **left** through the successive gates, past post 268, and follow the track (Beechen Lane) for 1⅓ miles to post 281 at a T-junction.

⑤ ► Turn **left**, pass through the gate and keep **ahead**, later going through another gate and then over a bridge, after which the track gently ascends to a junction.
► Bear **right** and in 35 yards go **left** at a fork, up to the road (B3056). **Cross** and keep ahead on a grassy path to a crossing track.

32 Short Walks Made Easy

Top left: Shetland pony with 'tail mark'
Above: gorse
Left: The Ridge track
Below: Scots pine cone

The Ridge — Trig point — Bolton's Bench

4 miles — 4½ miles — 5 miles

Lyndhurst bus stop
Forestry England
Bolton's Bench car park

6 ▶ Turn **left** and follow the track along The Ridge. Later, pass the trig point over to the left and retrace your earlier steps back to the start.

☆ Pondhead Inclosure

The conservation area of Pondhead Inclosure is a woodland site that has not been grazed by animals for several centuries, resulting in a rich variety of flora (notably bluebells in spring), birds and butterflies. It is carefully sustained by coppicing, the work carried out by volunteers from the Pondhead Conservation Trust.

Walk 3 Lyndhurst

WALK 4

BURLEY

CATCH A BUS

OS information

SU 211031
Explorer OL22

Distance
4.25 miles / 6.8 km

Time
2¼ hours

Start/Finish
Burley

Parking BH24 4AB
Burley car park or the adjacent Queen's Head car park, both pay & display

Public toilets
Burley car park

Cafés/pubs
Burley

Terrain
Pavement and country lanes; woodland tracks

Hilliness
One gentle ascent ❶ to ❷ and descent into Burley Street

Footwear
Winter 🥾
Spring/Summer/Autumn 👟

Public transport
Bus service 125, between Christchurch and Ringwood, using Queen's Head bus stop at 🚶: morebus.co.uk

Burley is a popular Forest village, with cafés, pubs and souvenir shops lining its main street. Notorious for its association with witchcraft, it was once a renowned haunt for smugglers. And just outside the village is the location of what is reputed to have been a dragon's lair. Away from the hustle and bustle of the village centre, there is some lovely countryside to be enjoyed. This circular walk takes you around the edge of Burley and the nearby hamlet of Burley Street.

Local legend According to local folklore, Burley Beacon – a large, peaceful grassy meadow passed after ❶ – was once the location of a dragon's den. The creature, notorious for 'doing much mischief among men and cattle', flew every morning to Bisterne, a village about 3 miles to the west, there demanding a pail of milk. Eventually a knight, Sir Maurice Berkeley, lord of the manor of Bisterne, killed it. Known as the Bisterne Dragon, it's said that the knight fought it throughout the Forest, the dragon finally dying just outside Lyndhurst, where its corpse formed the Bolton's Bench mound (see Walk 3). It is possible the beast was, in fact, a wild boar.

Accessibility
The wooden barriers on Church Lane before ❼ may not be passable by all wheelchairs, so remain on Chapel Lane from ❻, pushchair friendly throughout

Dogs
Welcome, but keep on leads along lanes and at Castle Hill. No stiles

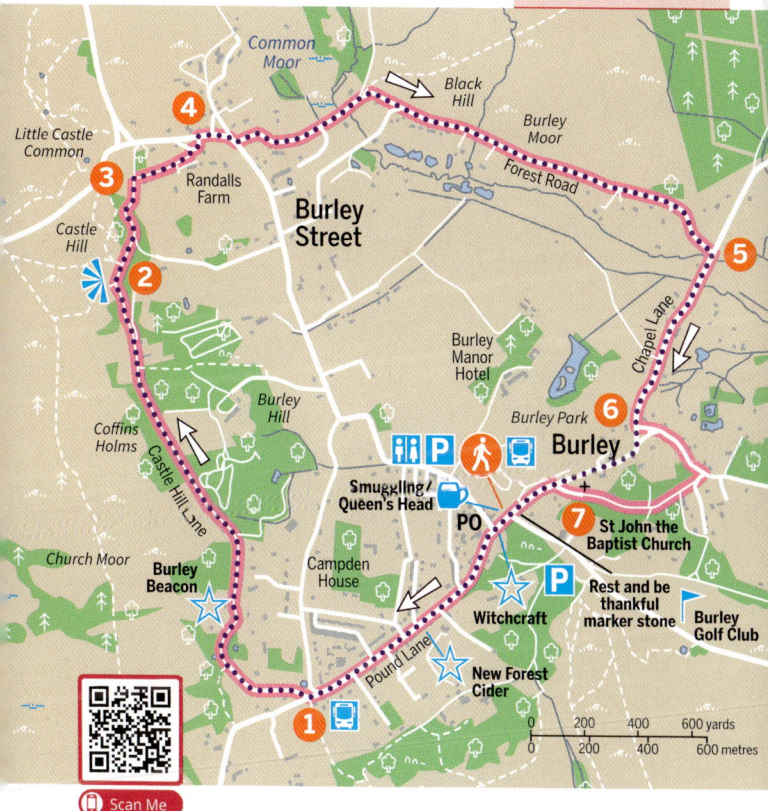

Walk 4 Burley 35

STORIES BEHIND THE WALK

☕ **Smuggling** The 17th-century Queen's Head was once a favourite smugglers' haunt. During renovations a hidden cellar, full of pistols, bottles and coins, was discovered beneath the floor of the Stable Bar. The New Forest's network of paths and tracks provided ideal cover for moving contraband inland from the coast. Ridley Wood to the north of Burley served as a black market for these goods.

☆ **Witchcraft**
During the 1950s, Burley was home to a 'white' witch called Sybil Leek. She used to walk around the village in a black cape with her pet jackdaw, Hotfoot Jackson, perched on her shoulder. She subsequently moved to America where she continued writing books on the occult and astrology. One of the village shops, A Coven of Witches, where you can buy witchcraft paraphernalia, was named by her.

☆ Witchcraft ☆ New Forest Cider Burley Beacon ☆ 1 mile
☕ Queen's Head / Smuggling   ½ mile ❶
Pound Lane   Castle

Burley car park

➤ Turn **right** out of the car park past the Queen's Head, bearing **right** at the junction.
➤ Fork **left** at the war memorial along Pound Lane. Continue for ½ mile, passing New Forest Cider (left), to where the pavement ends opposite Castle Hill Lane.

❶ ➤ **Cross** the road to follow Castle Hill Lane for just over 1 mile, soon passing the grassy meadow of Burley Beacon, ascending very gently past a number of large properties to reach Castle Hill fort at the top.

36 Short Walks Made Easy

☆ **New Forest Cider** Passed on the first leg of the walk, New Forest Cider's products are made in the traditional way using English apples from their own orchards, and elsewhere. Visitors can try unpasteurised, real cider direct from the barrels. Tea, coffee and other refreshments are available too. Apple pressing takes place in October and November, and there's also a Craft Cider Festival Weekend in October when you can watch cider making using vintage presses (newforestcider.co.uk).

Castle Hill Also passed on the route of the walk at its highest point is Castle Hill, the site of an Iron Age hillfort. It has a single rampart and ditch and covers an area of five acres. Although the site is overgrown, you can still enjoy the extensive views from the top. A waymarked route runs round the reserve (please keep dogs on leads).

2 ▸ Pause to admire the views.
▸ Resume by keeping **ahead**, down the track for 300 yards to a fork, ignoring an earlier track joining from the right.

3 ▸ At the fork bear **right**, walking down past Randalls Farm, to reach a small triangular green in Burley Street in 300 yards. Fork **right** to the village road.

4 ▸ **Cross** to the opposite pavement and head **right**, passing Coach Hill Lane.
▸ Take the next **left**, Forest Road. After crossing a bridge the road bends right, heading across open heathland for ¾ mile to a Y-junction at its end.

NATURE NOTES

Much of the New Forest National Park is open-access countryside – known as open forest – such as the grassland alongside Forest Road ④ to ⑤. You have the right to walk and explore freely on foot in these areas, although it's often easier to stick to the footpaths, bridleways and cycle tracks.

Holly trees and oak trees are found along the wooded track between ① and ②. In autumn, rowan trees along this track bear lots of scarlet berries. The woodland is ideal habitat for jays, one of Britain's most exotic-looking birds and the most colourful member of the crow family.

Small pools on the heathland alongside Forest Road, ④ to ⑤, provide welcome watering holes for ponies and cattle, and these ponds and the runnels that top them up are home to darting damselflies, such as the southern damselfly, on the wing from May to August.

Taking a wagon ride with rare-breed horses is an enjoyable way to see the local area. These leave from the coach park adjoining the village car park (burleynewforest.co.uk).

Forest Road

2½ miles

3 miles

⑤ ▬ Turn **right** at the junction along Chapel Lane, being mindful of any traffic, and follow it for ⅓ mile to the turning for Beechwood Lane.

⑥ ▬ Turn **left** along Beechwood Lane and in about 300 yards go **right** along gravelled Church Lane.
▬ Ignore turnings and keep **ahead** through lovely woodland, passing two barriers to reach St John the Baptist Church (built in 1838, with some striking stained-glass windows).

38 Short Walks Made Easy

Above: oak
Below: rowan berries

Top: southern damselfly
Bottom: jay

Chapel Lane

5

⋮ 3½ miles

6

Beechwood Lane

6 Keep ahead on Chapel Lane

Church Lane

⋮ 4 miles

St John the Baptist Church ✚

7

Queen's Head/ Smuggling

Burley car park

7 ▬ Keep ahead to the end of Church Lane then turn **left** at the junction back to the start.

Did you know? On the roadside just uphill from the Queen's Head is an unusual 'Rest and be thankful' marker stone, also inscribed 'Peace restored 27th March 1802'. This refers to the restoration of peace by the Treaty of Amiens in 1802, which temporarily ended hostilities between France and Britain.

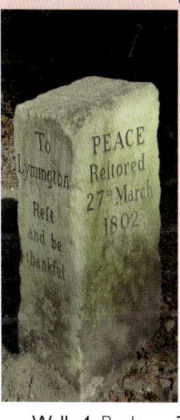

Opposite (clockwise): sedge warbler; heathland pool near Burley; white admiral; laver spire shells (mudsnails); Lepe mudflats
This page (clockwise): black-tailed godwit; honeysuckle; oak

WALK 5

BROCKENHURST

Surrounded by beautiful woodland, heath and grassland, the lovely village of Brockenhurst, with its free-roaming ponies and donkeys, makes an ideal walking base. Moreover, since it's on the mainline railway from London Waterloo to Weymouth you can leave the car behind and enjoy a traffic-free trip into the heart of the New Forest. There is good walking to be had in all directions and you'll find much of historic interest, with lots of places to eat and drink in the village.

OS information	
SU 300019 Explorer OL22	
Distance	4.3 miles/7km
Time	2¼ hours
Start/Finish	Brockenhurst
Parking	SO42 7TW Brockenhurst Station car park; alternatively, Brookley Road car park, SO42 7RD
Public toilets	At Brockenhurst Station and Brookley Road car parks
Cafés/pubs	Brockenhurst
Terrain	Village pavement and gravel tracks
Hilliness	Level throughout
Footwear	Year round
Public transport	South Western Railway services between London Waterloo and Weymouth: southwesternrailway.com. Bus services from Southampton, Hythe, Lymington, Ringwood and Wimborne: bluestarbus.co.uk; morebus.co.uk

Did you know? At the western end of Brookley Road (just after ①), you'll find a picturesque ford, the Watersplash. Just to the north is Meerut Road (crossed at ②), which adjoins the grassland known as Butts Lawn (lawn is a New Forest word for a grassy area used for grazing). The road was named in honour of the 7th Meerut Indian Army Division, whose soldiers were among the first casualties to arrive in the village in 1914.

Local legend Harry 'Brusher' Mills (1840–1905) was something of a legendary character in the area. He lived an austere life in a hut in the woods and was famed for catching snakes. It is estimated he caught around 30,000 in his lifetime. The nickname Brusher came about from his brushing or sweeping of the cricket pitch before a game. The Snakecatcher pub in Brockenhurst is named after him. He is buried in the graveyard at St Nicholas's Church where his headstone can be found.

Walk 5 Brockenhurst

STORIES BEHIND THE WALK

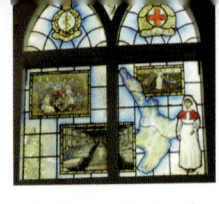

St Nicholas's Church This is the oldest church in the New Forest, with a great yew tree that is over 1,000 years old. Here, you'll also find the graves of New Zealand soldiers killed in World War I. In 1914, the War Office designated Brockenhurst a key hospital centre, with 3,500 troops from India and 21,000 from New Zealand treated here. A memorial stained-glass window in the church, a gift from the people of New Zealand, was unveiled in 2016.

New Zealand Cemetery The St Nicholas's churchyard contains 93 graves of New Zealand soldiers killed in World War I. The original white crosses were replaced in 1924 by engraved headstones and the impressive memorial cross was erected in 1927. An annual ANZAC memorial service is held here in April. Brockenhurst itself also lost many local men: 79 out of a population that numbered only 2,000 in 1914.

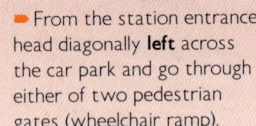

Brockenhurst Station — St Saviour's Church — ① Watersplash (ford) — ½ mile — Meerut Road — ② — Butts Lawn — 1 mile — Black

- From the station entrance head diagonally **left** across the car park and go through either of two pedestrian gates (wheelchair ramp).
- Turn **left** then first **right** along Avenue Road to reach the B3055.
- **Cross** the road, go **right**, and then **left** along The Rise to a junction opposite St Saviour's Church.

① - Turn **right** along the pavement passing the Watersplash at end of Brookley Road.
- Keep **ahead** along Rhinefield Road and in ¼ mile, at a gravel path intersection just before a road junction, fork **right** to Meerut Road.

44   Short Walks Made Easy

✛ St Saviour's Church

Situated in the village centre, not far from the Watersplash, St Saviour's Church is a striking example of late Victorian Gothic architecture. The original intention of the Walker-Munro family was to build a private chapel for their residence, Rhinefield House, situated two miles west of Brockenhurst, but the then vicar suggested a new and larger church on village land they owned. Work started in 1895 and the opening ceremony was held ten years later.

☆ North Lodge gatehouse

This French Renaissance-style 19th-century gatehouse at the north entrance to Brockenhurst Park Estate can be found just a few minutes' walk along Mill Lane from the station. The estate was bought in the 18th century by Edward Morant. He rebuilt the house as a large Georgian mansion (later demolished) and laid out the avenues in the grounds. The park is privately owned, although North Lodge is rented out as a holiday let.

1½ miles | **3** Short detour to Bolderford Bridge (right) | 2 miles

2 ▶ **Cross** the road and take the gravel path opposite for almost 1 mile over a large grassy area called Black Knowl to a path junction (post 264) at its far corner.
▶ A brief detour **right** leads to the Lymington River at pretty Bolderford Bridge.

3 ▶ At post 264 go **left** (or keep **ahead** after detouring) along a wide gravel cycle track to a barrier at the end.
▶ Keep **ahead** along the access road past Ober Corner car park for 250 yards to a turning on the right to Aldridge Hill Campsite.

NATURE NOTES

The great yew tree outside St Nicholas's church is over 1,000 years old. It has a girth of more than 20 feet and its larger branches extend 30 feet or more from its now-hollow trunk.

Silver birch trees are characteristic of the wooded heath of Black Knowl, ❷ to ❸. The pale bark sheds tissue paper-like layers and on mature trees the trunk develops darker, diamond-shaped fissures. The tree is a symbol of purity.

The hornbeam has serrated leaves and its fruit (a very small nut) is attached to a three-lobed bract.

During the autumn pigs are allowed onto the Forest to feed on the fallen acorns, which can be poisonous to ponies and cattle if eaten to excess. It is referred to as the 'pannage' season (see Walk 3).

Buzzards are the birds of prey most frequently seen and heard here. Typically they may be observed soaring on thermals rising over the heathland plains; their cry is a cat-like mewing.

Brockenhurst Beach (pictured below) is the local name for a spot on the Lymington River near the Balmer Lawn Hotel. The water here is quite shallow, so it's good for children to paddle and splash about in. There's a free car park too.

❹ ➤ Turn **right**, crossing Ober Water, and keep **ahead** to a white cottage at the end.
➤ Pass to its **left** and soon fork **left** opposite a wooden shed.
➤ Follow the path through trees, over an Ober Water footbridge, and keep **ahead** to a road.

❺ ➤ Bear **right** and follow the road to Beachern Wood car park.
➤ **Cross** the car park and head diagonally **left** over grass to a road (not far from a junction, left).
➤ Stay on the lane to the junction and go **right** to a track on the left.

Short Walks Made Easy

1,000-year-old yew tree at St Nicholas's Church

Acorns

Above: pigs rooting
Below: yew berries

6 ➤ Go **straight across** to continue on a gravel track (residential access drive).
➤ Follow this for almost 1 mile and then, nearing a road, fork **left** past a barrier, continuing beside a road to Armstrong Lane on the left.

7 ➤ **Cross** the road to cycle post 234 and follow a gravel path across Culverley Green, passing a school at the end.
➤ Go **over** a zebra crossing and turn **left** and then **right** along Avenue Road back to the start.

Walk 5 Brockenhurst 47

WALK 6

BOLDRE

This walk starts at Boldre's lovely old church, which is set atop a small hill above the Lymington River valley, well away from the village itself. Do go inside to learn more about its famous 18th-century vicar, William Gilpin. The walk is a peaceful and varied circuit through Roydon Woods Nature Reserve, crossing the Lymington River twice, and passing the Red Lion pub in the village. There is a shortcut option.

OS information	
SZ 324993 Explorer OL22	
Distance	3.9 miles/6.25km
Time	2 hours
Start/Finish	Church of St John the Baptist, Boldre
Parking	SO41 5PG Church car park, signed off Church Lane
Public toilets	None
Cafés/pubs	Red Lion, Boldre
Terrain	Footpaths, tracks and country lanes. Bridleways likely to be muddy after wet weather
Hilliness	Gently undulating, with one short descent and one moderate ascent
Footwear	Winter / Spring/Summer/Autumn

Public transport

Nearest bus stop at Battramsley Cross on the A337, 0.6 mile west of ⑤ (the Red Lion, Boldre), for bus service 6 between Southampton and Lymington: bluestarbus.co.uk

Accessibility

In dry conditions, powered wheelchairs and all-terrain pushchairs using shortcut from ④ to return to 🚶.

Dogs

Welcome but keep on a lead in Roydon Woods (deer and livestock) and along country lanes. No stiles

Did you know? In 1787, the First Fleet left Portsmouth to found the penal colony of New South Wales, Australia. It was commanded by Admiral Arthur Phillip of Lyndhurst with the Reverend Richard Johnson, curate of Boldre, as chaplain. Johnson built the first wattle-and-daub church in New South Wales. His Bible and prayer book reside in the replacement church of St Philip's, Sydney.

Local legend According to local folklore, the Red Lion in Boldre is named after the Stratford Lyon [sic], supposedly a giant red lion with huge stag-like antlers, pulled from the ground by a local verderer, John Stratford, in the late 14th or early 15th century.

Walk 6 Boldre 49

STORIES BEHIND THE WALK

✝ Church of St John the Baptist

In its tranquil hilltop setting, this is one of the loveliest of the New Forest churches. It dates back to the late 11th century although there have been many alterations over the years. In the past it was the mother (most senior) church in the area, its extensive parish containing the two then 'chapels' of Brockenhurst and Lymington. In the entrance porch there's a charming poem about the church on the noticeboard, which describes it well.

☆ Millennium Window

Commissioned by Boldre Parochial Church Council to mark the millennium, this beautiful window in the church was designed and engraved by Tracey Sheppard. It depicts the church in its rural setting with various flora and fauna, each with a symbolic Christian meaning. The oak, for example, illustrates the strength of the Church and is also a tree of life and symbol of resurrection.

Entrance to Roydon Woods Nature Reserve (Dilton Gardens, right)

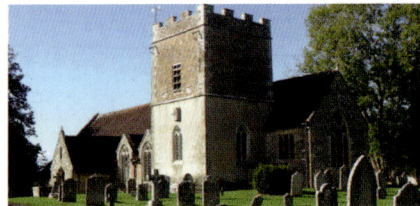

✝ Church of St John the Baptist; Millennium Window

Reverend William Gilpin; HMS *Hood*

Heywood Farm

½ mile

Roydon Nature

Church car park
- Follow the enclosed footpath out of the car park at its far **right-hand** corner.
- At a T-junction (Heywood Farm) turn **left** along a vehicle track for ½ mile. Keep **ahead/left** at the first fork to another in 50 yards.

❶
- Fork **left** along the track to the entrance gate into Roydon Woods Nature Reserve in 300 yards (drive to Dilton Gardens, right).
- Keep **ahead** into the reserve and follow the track through woodland for ½ mile to a fingerposted T-Junction.

⭐ Reverend William Gilpin

Vicar of Boldre from 1777 until his death in 1804, William Gilpin was originally from Cumbria, and headmaster of Cheam School (Berkshire) for 25 years. He was offered the position at Boldre by one of his former pupils. An enlightened educationalist, building a local school, he was also an artist of distinction, credited with the founding of the 'picturesque' movement, and a renowned writer. His chest tomb in the graveyard bears an inscription composed by Gilpin himself.

⭐ HMS *Hood*

Inside the church there's a memorial to HMS *Hood* (and a painting of it too), a battle cruiser – the largest warship afloat when commissioned in 1920 – sunk by the German battleship, *Bismarck*, in 1941. Of the crew of 1,418 men, only three survived. Among those who died was Vice Admiral LE Holland, who had been a regular worshipper at Boldre for many years. A service is held here every May in memory of the ship's company.

1 mile — Woods Reserve — ② — Roydon Manor (off to the right) — **1½ miles** — Footbridge, Lymington River — ③

② ➤ Go **left** and follow the track downhill to cross a footbridge over the Lymington River. Roydon Manor can be seen across the grass (right).
➤ Continue to a five-bar metal gate and T-junction (potentially muddy) in 250 yards.

③ ➤ Pass through the gate and go **left**, keeping **ahead** at a turning on the right in 200 yards.
➤ Continue along the track to leave the nature reserve through a gate, keeping **forwards** along a lane to a crossroads in ¼ mile.

NATURE NOTES

Roydon Woods Nature Reserve is in the care of the Hampshire & Isle of Wight Wildlife Trust. In spring, look out for wildflowers such as wood anemones, bluebells, stitchwort, marsh marigold and wood spurge.

If you're lucky (and keep very quiet!) you may spot deer. There are five species in the New Forest: fallow, roe, red, sika and muntjac. The name 'fallow' is derived from the Old English 'falu', meaning spotted, a reference to the deer's coat in summer.

Among the woodland birds you might hear or see are great spotted woodpeckers, treecreepers and nuthatches, while there also is a good population of tawny owls.

The rides and clearings in Roydon Woods provide habitat for several woodland butterflies: the pearl-bordered fritillary in spring, and in high summer the silver-washed fritillary and white admiral. Dog violet is the caterpillar foodplant for both fritillaries, while white admiral larvae feed on honeysuckle.

Above: dog violets
Opposite top: tawny owl
Opposite bottom: silver-washed fritillary

Exit from Roydon Woods Nature Reserve — 2 miles

Shortcut back to church along Church Lane (left) — 4 — 2½ miles

4
- For a shortcut back to 🚶, turn **left** and keep **forwards** on Church Lane for ½ mile.
- Otherwise, keep **ahead** to the next lane junction.

- Stay **ahead/left** here and follow the lane for ½ mile to a green, left, (Perkins' Piece — see information panel) and road junction, Red Lion opposite.

Short Walks Made Easy

Above: fallow deer, doe and fawn

Church of St John the Baptist;
Millennium Window;
Reverend William Gilpin;
HMS *Hood*

Red Lion

Boldre Bridge, Lymington River

Rodlease Farm (left), Plant Yard nursery (right)

3½ miles

3 miles

Church car park

5 ► Turn **left**, soon crossing Boldre Bridge over Lymington River.

► At the junction just beyond, keep **left** on Rodlease Lane and follow it for ⅓ mile to the entrance drives to Rodlease Farm (left) and Plant Yard nursery (right).

6 ► Turn **right** onto a track, passing the Plant Yard nursery over to the left, and follow it uphill through trees for ⅓ mile to a lane at the top.

► On reaching the lane, turn **left** back to the church car park.

Walk **6** Boldre

WALK 7

BEAULIEU TO BUCKLER'S HARD

Set beside the river that shares its name, the attractive village of Beaulieu (whose name, appropriately enough, means beautiful place) dates back to the 13th century when Cistercian monks founded an abbey. Famously, the National Motor Museum is located here. This easy out-and-back walk takes you from Beaulieu to the picturesque 18th-century hamlet of Buckler's Hard, once a busy shipbuilding centre providing ships for Nelson's Navy, now a tranquil and popular haven for yachties.

OS information
SU 386021 Explorer OL22
Distance 4.8 miles/7.7km
Time 2½ hours
Start/Finish Beaulieu
Parking SO42 7PJ Beaulieu car park; SO42 7ZN: large car park at the National Motor Museum
Public toilets Beaulieu car park; Buckler's Hard
Cafés/pubs Beaulieu; Buckler's Hard
Terrain Wide gravel track, with short optional riverside gravel paths and boardwalks
Hilliness Level throughout

Short Walks Made Easy

Did you know? Beaulieu served as a top-secret training establishment for agents of the Special Operations Executive (SOE) during World War II. Over 3,000 were trained here before undertaking daring and dangerous missions behind enemy lines. Visit the Secret Army Exhibition to learn more about their training at Beaulieu and how the agents' courageous actions helped bring about victory in the war (beaulieu.co.uk/attractions/secret-army-exhibition).

Local legend Some years ago, builders working on an old Beaulieu Estate property found a solitary old boot beneath the floorboards under the original entrance to the property. It has been suggested this was hidden there to prevent evil crossing the threshold. Items were purposely secreted in such places either to ward off evil spirits or bestow good luck and fertility upon the occupants.

Footwear
Year round

 Public transport
Bus service 112 between Lymington and Hythe, Tuesdays and Thursdays only; New Forest Tour bus, Green Route, July to mid-September only: morebus.co.uk

Accessibility
Suitable throughout for powered wheelchairs and pushchairs

Dogs
Welcome but keep on leads where signed, including along riverside diversions. No stiles

Walk 7 Beaulieu to Buckler's Hard

STORIES BEHIND THE WALK

Beaulieu The mill pond was created by the monks who built a dam across Beaulieu River to power their corn mill. Following Henry VIII's dissolution of the monasteries in the 1530s, Beaulieu was sold to the 1st Earl of Southampton, ancestor of the present Lord Montagu. The

estate has been in the family ever since. As well as the National Motor Museum, other attractions include Palace House (once the Beaulieu Abbey gatehouse and now the Montagu family home), the Abbey ruins and Beaulieu Parish Church, formerly the monks' refectory. The gardens can be explored via a network of paths.

☆ Bailey's Hard

The walk takes you past Brickyard Cottage and Brickworks House at Bailey's Hard. This was the location of a former brickworks, built in 1790. It closed in 1935 and the house is now a private residence (available as a holiday let). Bailey's Hard is also where the first naval vessel, HMS *Salisbury*, was built on the river and launched in 1698.

Bailey's Hard (left)

The Beaulieu Bakehouse; Pallets Montagu Arms Hotel

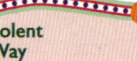

Fire Station · ½ mile · Solent Way · 1 mile · Gate to north loop

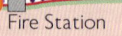

Beaulieu car park

- Facing the toilet block, take the gravel path to the **right**, passing The Beaulieu Bakehouse to reach High Street.
- Go **left** to the main road and bear **right** to the turning just after the Montagu Arms Hotel.

① ▶ Turn **right** along Fire Station Lane, signed Solent Way. Pass the fire station and keep **ahead** on a gravel track to go through a gate in 150 yards.
- Stroll down the track for ⅔ mile, passing meadows and through a copse to a barrier.

Short Walks Made Easy

☆ Duke's Bath House
Passed as you reach Buckler's Hard, this quaint thatched cottage was built by George, Duke of Montagu, in 1760 for his son who suffered from arthritis. Salt water was considered a beneficial treatment – a pool in the garden was filled with river water in which to bathe. This cottage, too, is now rented out as a holiday let.

🏛️ 🌊 Buckler's Hard
Founded in the 1720s by the 2nd Duke of Montagu, Buckler's Hard was intended as a trading port but developed into a busy shipbuilding centre, with timber readily available from the surrounding New Forest. It became famous for the ships it built for Nelson's Navy, including three that took part in the Battle of Trafalgar. Visit the Maritime Museum to learn more, and have a look in an 18th-century worker's cottage. You can also enjoy a river cruise between Easter and the end of October.

North loop exit | Entrance to south loop | Keeping Marsh bird hide (left) | | Buckler's Hard Yacht Harbour (left) | Duke's Bath House
— | ❹ 1½ miles | ❺ South loop exit | 2 miles | | ❻ Solent Way ☆ | Beaulieu River Quay

❷ ▸ After the barrier, jink **left** then **right** with the track, past the turning (left) to Brickyard Cottage and Bailey's Hard, with New Forest Activities Centre (right).
▸ Keep **ahead** where a drive joins from the left and bend **right** to a junction (signed Buckler's Hard).

❸ ▸ Turn **left** for 100 yards to a gate on the left.
▸ Go through the gate to follow the riverside diversion north loop, rejoining main route in 350 yards.
▸ Turn **left** to continue to the next riverside diversion – south loop – in ⅓ mile.

Walk 7 Beaulieu to Buckler's Hard

NATURE NOTES

The route taken on this walk is part of the Solent Way – a 60-mile long-distance path between Christchurch and Emsworth – and takes you through the heart of the Beaulieu Estate and the North Solent National Nature Reserve. Information panels along the way tell you more about the different habitats, including ancient woodland and grassland, mudflats and salt marshes, a key feature of the Beaulieu River. Two short loops in the path allow walkers to enjoy riverside stretches with lovely views.

Reeds are an important wetland habitat, frequented by birds such as reed bunting, present year round, and reed warbler and sedge warbler, both of which are summer visitors. Reeds are also a sustainable crop, which can be harvested early in the year for use in thatching. As roof thatch, reed can last up to 50 years, a lot longer than straw.

The millpond is a haven for mute swans, greylag and Canada geese, and ducks, such as mallard and shelduck. The Beaulieu River is also home to heron and little egret.

Buckler's Hard

The Captain's Table

7 — 2½ miles — Beaulieu River Quay — Duke's Bath House — Buckler's Hard Yacht Harbour (right) — 3 miles — Solent Way — Keeping Marsh bird hide (right) — 3½ miles

4
- Go through the gate on the **left** to follow this loop past a viewing platform.
- On rejoining the main route, go **left** for a few paces to a gate on the left.

5
- Go through the gate and along a boardwalk to visit Keeping Marsh bird hide.
- Retrace steps and turn **left** to continue on the main track. At a boatyard, go **straight across** the access drive (Buckler's Hard Yacht Harbour, left).

Above: shelduck
Below: reed bunting

Top: Beaulieu Mill Pond
Bottom: greylag goose and goslings

Bailey's Hard
(right)

The Beaulieu Bakehouse

|← 4 miles →| |← 4½ miles →|

Solent Way

6 ▸ Continue **ahead** along the gravel path, bending **right** near the waterfront to pass the Duke's Bath House, right.
▸ Carry on to a jetty then go **right**, uphill, to explore Buckler's Hard. Museum and tearoom are at the top.

7 ▸ Retrace your outward steps, omitting the riverside diversions (or not!).
▸ Approaching Beaulieu, after the gate across the track, turn **left** through a gate by a hotel car park. Wind with the enclosed path to the High Street, crossing **straight over** to return to the car park.

Beaulieu car park

Walk 7 Beaulieu to Buckler's Hard

Opposite (clockwise): The Snakecatcher, Brockenhurst; The Red Lion, Boldre; The Lookout, Lepe; Trusty Servant Inn, Minstead; The Beaulieu Bakehouse
This page (clockwise): Queen's Head, Burley; The Cider Pantry, Burley; New Forest Heritage Centre, Lyndhurst

WALK 8

LEPE

Situated on the coast in the south-east corner of the New Forest National Park, Lepe has beaches, wildflower meadows and fine views from the pine-fringed cliffs across the Solent to the Isle of Wight. Lepe played an important role in the D-Day landings – you can see some of the foreshore remains of the amphibious training operations here. This walk, known as the Lepe Loop, combines coast and countryside, and nearby Exbury Gardens are well worth a visit too.

OS information
SZ 455985 Explorer OL22
Distance 4.5 miles/7.25km
Time 2½ hours
Start/Finish Lepe Country Park
Parking SO45 1AD Lepe Country Park car park
Public toilets Lepe Country Park
Cafés/pubs The Lookout, Lepe Country Park; restaurant and café at Exbury Gardens

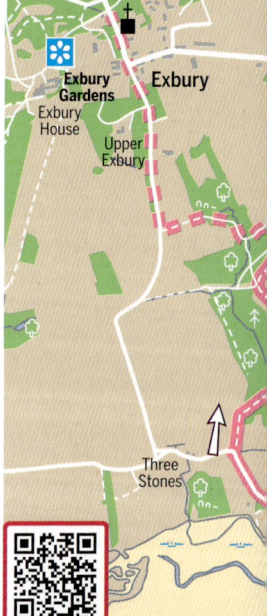

Did you know? Lepe's lighthouse – or Beaulieu Millennium Beacon, as it's officially known – was built to mark the entrance to Beaulieu River and named to commemorate the year 2000. It is located in the private grounds of Lepe House, in the Beaulieu Estate, but can be seen from the coast path on this walk. The 25-foot-high traditional-style lighthouse assists boats sailing in and out of the river, which runs alongside the south-eastern shores of the Beaulieu Estate. The estuary is privately owned by the Montagu family. Atop the lighthouse is a weathervane which includes the three red diamonds that are the symbol of the Beaulieu Estate.

Local legend In the 16th and 17th centuries, Lepe was a haunt for smugglers shipping contraband from the Isle of Wight out through the New Forest via the secluded channel of the Dark Water.

Terrain
Clifftop paths; sand and shingle beach; field and woodland paths and tracks; quiet country lanes

Hilliness
Mostly level with gentle undulations

Footwear
Winter 🥾
Spring/Summer/Autumn

Public transport
None

Accessibility
🚶 to ①, the country park paths and tracks, and Exbury Gardens are wheelchair and pushchair friendly

Dogs
Welcome but observe the restrictions on beach access

STORIES BEHIND THE WALK

☆ **Watch House** In the 18th century, Lepe was a small village with a harbour used for shipbuilding. This narrow part of the Solent became much used by smugglers, so during the following century coastguards were installed here to combat the illegal trade. Cottages were built to house the Chief Preventative Officer and his boatman, and the Watch House on the shore contained their wooden rowing boat.

✺ **Exbury Gardens** Exbury Estate was bought in 1919 by the banker Lionel Nathan de Rothschild, who remodelled the house and created the beautiful 200-acre woodland garden, famous for its colourful collection of camellias, rhododendrons and azaleas. There are miles of woodland paths to walk here and a popular steam railway. During World War II the house was requisitioned and used for the planning and operation of the D-Day landings. It is well worth extending the walk to visit the gardens – ¾ mile each way (exbury.co.uk).

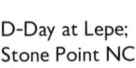

➤ Begin at the beachfront car park and, with the sea on your left, follow the coast road pavement across the Dark Water bridge.

➤ As the coast road bears away right, keep **ahead** on a gravel path below it to reach the Watch House.

❶ ➤ On the far side of the Watch House continue along boardwalk, passing below the lighthouse and then along shingle beach below Lepe House to a fingerpost (right).

☆ Stone Point NCI

The National Coastwatch Institution (NCI) is a voluntary organisation set up in 1994 to restore a lookout service along Britain's shores after many small coastguard stations closed. Each lookout is staffed by dedicated volunteers, who keep a daylight watch throughout the year. The wood-clad unit at Stone Point was installed on the clifftop at Lepe in 2022.

☆ D-Day at Lepe

Lepe was a cornerstone in the preparations for D-Day during World War II, with three important roles: firstly, as a departure point for troops, vehicles and supplies; secondly, as a construction site for Mulberry Harbours, huge concrete caissons (boxes) floated across the English Channel; and thirdly, as the base for the PLUTO oil pipeline, laid in support of Operation Overlord. Today, there's plenty of evidence of wartime activity to be seen along the beach eastwards from the car park.

❹ 2 miles

❸ 1½ miles

Beach walk

❷ ▸ If the tide permits, **carry on** along the beach below low cliffs then an oak-fringed foreshore to meet a lane.
▸ If the tide is too high, fork **right** at the fingerpost up to a lane and turn **left** along it for ¾ mile to meet the shore.

❸ ▸ From the beach, bear **left** along the lane. Where it bends left by a gravelled area (right) in 300 yards, turn **right** and follow a fingerposted path into trees.
▸ Continue through woodland to a plank bridge and wooden gate in ¼ mile.

NATURE NOTES

The large grassy area along the country park's clifftop is lined with Monterey pine trees – a species native to California and Mexico – and there are benches on which to relax and enjoy the views across the Solent to the Isle of Wight.

The Dark Water is a reed-fringed channel, with marshland and wet woodland, passed soon after 🚶. This is ideal habitat for all kinds of wading birds and wildfowl, but you may be lucky enough to spot a marsh harrier, and spoonbills are occasional visitors.

Estuarine mudflats and salt marsh can be seen in the Beaulieu River, which empties into the Solent near Lepe. These are rich feeding grounds for overwintering birds such as redshank, easily recognised by their red legs, and the dark-bellied Brent geese.

On the beach itself, you'll find yellow-horned poppy and sea rocket. Commonly seen feeding on seaweed, see if you can find any tiny laver spire shells, also known as mudsnails.

Inland, in spring, the woodland paths are lined with primroses.

Brent goose

5 Detour (left) ¾ mile each way to **Exbury Gardens** | 2½ miles | 3 miles | **6** East Hill Farm

4 ▪ Go through the gate into an open field and turn **left** along its edge.
▪ Bear round to the **right** at the far end and keep **ahead** through two gates, soon reaching a fingerpost and T-Junction.

5 ▪ Turn **right**, along the field edge, to a road in ¼ mile.
▪ Go **straight across** and stay on the gravel access track (later surfaced) to East Hill Farm in almost ¾ mile.

Top left: marsh harrier
Bottom left: salt marsh
Above: yellow-horned poppy
Below: sea rocket

3½ miles

4 miles

D-Day at Lepe;
Stone Point NCI

6 ▪ Just past a white cottage (left), keep **ahead** on a narrow footpath which bends right and heads down to a T-junction.
▪ Turn **right** on a path that soon bends left then emerges from the wood.
▪ Keep **ahead** across four fields, gently descending to a bridge.

7 ▪ Over the bridge, bear **left** up to the field corner. Go through a kissing-gate (information panel).
▪ Continue across grass past pines (right) to another kissing-gate leading into a car park.
▪ Follow the drive out to the road and go **left** back to the start.

Lepe Country Park car park

Walk 8 Lepe 67

WALK 9

SWAY

Located in the south of the New Forest, Sway is a large village best known for its tower, a folly, which is visible from afar. Although not a tourist hotspot, you'll find a choice of good pubs and shops here as well as some lovely walking nearby. Moreover, the village is on the mainline railway, just five minutes from Brockenhurst. To the north of Sway is a former railway line, now a very pleasant path used ❹ to ❺.

OS information
SZ 275984 Explorer OL22
Distance 4 miles/6.5km
Time 2 hours
Start/Finish Sway
Parking SO41 6BA Sway Railway Station car park; alternatively, Forestry England's Longslade Bottom car park at ❸ or Longslade View car park between ❺ and ❻
Public toilets None
Cafés/pubs Sway
Terrain Village roads; woodland and heathland paths and tracks
Hilliness Gently undulating
Footwear Winter Spring/Summer/Autumn

Did you know? In the autumn, ponies are rounded up in what are called 'drifts' under the supervision of their owners and the agisters (employees of the verderers), who assist in the management of stock in the New Forest. A number of these drifts are held over a couple of months or so. At this time ponies are 'tail-marked' (see Walk 3) and checked over. Members of the public are not encouraged to attend drifts because of the risks involved with ponies being driven, often at speed. Car parks (such as the Longslade ones on this walk) may be closed for part of a day when a drift is to take place.

Public transport

South Western Railway services between London Waterloo and Weymouth: southwesternrailway.com. Bus services 120, between New Milton and Lymington, and X2, between Bournemouth and Lymington: morebus.co.uk

Accessibility

Powered wheelchairs and pushchairs to Longslade View car park at ⑥. Steep ramps onto/off embankment at ④ and ⑤. In dry conditions, all-terrain pushchairs on the heathland path ⑥ to ⑦.

Dogs

Welcome but keep on leads. No stiles

STORIES BEHIND THE WALK

☆ **Sway history** Sway has four mentions in the 1086 Domesday Book. Until the dissolution of the monasteries it was owned by three large churches: Quarr Abbey (on the Isle of Wight), Romsey Abbey and Christchurch Priory. St Luke's Church – passed on the walk – was built in 1839. The village expanded considerably with the arrival of the railway in 1888.

☆ **Sway Tower** This 218-foot-high tower, seen from a distance on this walk, is thought to be the world's tallest unreinforced concrete structure. It was built between 1879 and 1885 by Andrew Peterson, a barrister. He was also a philanthropist and took on the unemployed to build it. The tower is situated along a lane to the south of Sway, with a smaller prototype nearby to the north. Both are privately owned.

Today's railway
☆
Station Road — Mead East Road — ½ mile — Adlams Lane

Sway Railway Station car park

- From the railway station, walk along Station Approach to Station Road and turn **left**.
- Keep **forward** for 350 yards to fork **left** along Mead End Road, reaching Adlams Lane in another 350 yards.

1
- Fork **right** along Adlams Lane, which becomes a gravel track leading downhill to a gate.
- Go through this and the next gate **ahead** into Set Thorns Inclosure.
- Stay on the main track as it bends left and in 150 yards meet a broad crossways.

⭐ **Castleman's Corkscrew** A short stretch of the walk follows a disused railway line, now a shared-use path, which was once part of the Southampton and Dorchester Railway. It was planned by a Wimborne solicitor, Charles Castleman, with its meandering route earning it the nickname, Castleman's Corkscrew. Opened in 1847, from Brockenhurst it headed westwards via Ringwood, bypassing Bournemouth, which was then only a small village. The line closed in 1964.

⭐ **Today's railway** In 1888 a new mainline was opened from Brockenhurst through Bournemouth to Poole. By then Bournemouth had grown, like other seaside resorts in the country. The next stop on this new line from Brockenhurst was Sway. This part of the railway was difficult to build and a number of workers died during the construction. There are roads in Sway with place names like Manchester Road, thought to relate to the navvies' place of origin.

Set Thorns Inclosure — Wilverley Road — 1½ miles — 🅿 Longslade Bottom car park — Castleman's Corkscrew

❷ ➤ At the junction (cycle post 200), turn **right**.
➤ Keep **ahead** at all subsequent crossing paths and tracks for almost ½ mile to a gate and road.

❸ ➤ Go through the gate, cross the road and follow the path opposite, bearing **left** on the Longslade Bottom car park drive.
➤ Bend **right** then **left** with the drive through the car park, continuing past a barrier down a gravel path to a bridge.

❹ ➤ Fork **right** and climb the path onto the old railway line.
➤ Turn **right** for ½ mile to the next bridge.

Walk 9 Sway

NATURE NOTES

During the drift, some ponies have reflective collars fitted to help make them more visible at night. Sadly, animals are killed every year in road accidents – the maximum speed limit is 40mph on unfenced roads, but drivers should take great care at all times and reduce speed whenever animals are roadside.

Sweet chestnut trees can be seen alongside the track through Set Thorns Inclosure, after ❷. Hawthorns line the old railway line ❹ to ❺ and are laden with berries in late summer and autumn.

Ponies with reflective collars grazing near Longslade Bottom car park

The New Forest contains boggy wetland areas, such as Hincheslea Bog, which can be seen from the old railway between ❹ and ❺. Gravel causeways cross it, although they can flood at times.

❺ ▶ Just before the bridge, bear **right** down the embankment and bend **right** along a gravel track to Longslade View car park.

▶ Keep **forwards** to the road ahead.

❻ ▶ Cross the road to take the **leftmost** of two paths across the heath.

▶ Keep **ahead** at all crossing paths, maintaining direction for ½ mile to a railway bridge. (Sway Tower may be spotted in the distance.)

▶ Cross over the railway line and fork **right** to a road.

72 Short Walks Made Easy

There are four different types of heather that grow in the New Forest: most commonly, ling and bell heather, but also cross-leaved heath (above) and the rare Dorset heath. In late summer, the heathland blooms with carpets of purple heather, which make an attractive source of nectar for heathland butterflies such as the grayling and silver-studded blue.

Top: silver-studded blue
Middle: grayling
Bottom: bell heather

⑦ ▸ Turn **right**, passing the Hare & Hounds (left), going **right** again along Church Lane.
▸ In ¼ mile, turn **right** into a churchyard, pass the church (right) and go **left** through a car park to Station Road.
▸ Turn **right** and in 200 yards go **left** back to the station.

Local legend Published in 1847, *The Children of the New Forest* is a novel set in the pleasant countryside encountered on this walk. Its author, Frederick Marryat, a captain in the Royal Navy and acquaintance of Charles Dickens, lived in Sway.

WALK 10

KEYHAVEN

Although most of the New Forest coastline is inaccessible on foot, this beautiful stretch between the village of Keyhaven and the mouth of the Lymington River is ideal for walking. The route passes the Lymington-Keyhaven Marshes Nature Reserve and affords excellent views across the Solent to the Isle of Wight. It's a perfect ramble for some birdwatching, so take your binoculars. You can also walk, or take the ferry, out to the end of nearby Hurst Spit.

OS information
SZ 306914 Explorer OL22
Distance **Shorter loop**: 3.3 miles/5.3km **Longer loop**: 5.1 miles/8.2km **Hurst Spit**: 2.25 miles/3.6km (one way, with ferry return)
Time **Shorter loop**: 1½ hours **Longer loop**: 2½ hours **Hurst Spit**: 1¼ hours (each way)
Start/Finish Keyhaven
Parking SO41 0TP Keyhaven car park
Public toilets Keyhaven car park
Cafés/pubs The Gun Inn, Keyhaven, ⓦ; Chequers Inn, Lower Woodside, ④; Hurst Castle café
Terrain Seawall walkway; gravel tracks; quiet country lanes
Hilliness Level throughout
Footwear Year round

Public transport
Keyhaven to Hurst Castle ferry, daily (1 Apr to 31 Oct): hurstcastle.co.uk

Accessibility
Suitable for powered wheelchairs and all-terrain pushchairs using shortcut from ❷ to avoid narrow paths/steps ❸ to ❺, and along seawall ❺ to ❻ in both directions. Hurst Spit is shingle and not suited to wheelchairs or pushchairs

Dogs
Welcome, but under control at all times. No stiles

Did you know? Hurst Spit is a 1.4-mile-long shingle bank stretching out from the Hampshire coast into the Solent. On its east side it shelters large areas of salt marsh and mudflats. Over time the spit had become much reduced in volume so a stabilisation scheme took place in 1996–97. The Spit has to be reinforced from time to time, especially following storm damage. This is what caused a section of the East Wing wall at Hurst Castle to collapse a few years ago, when the sea exposed and undercut its foundations.

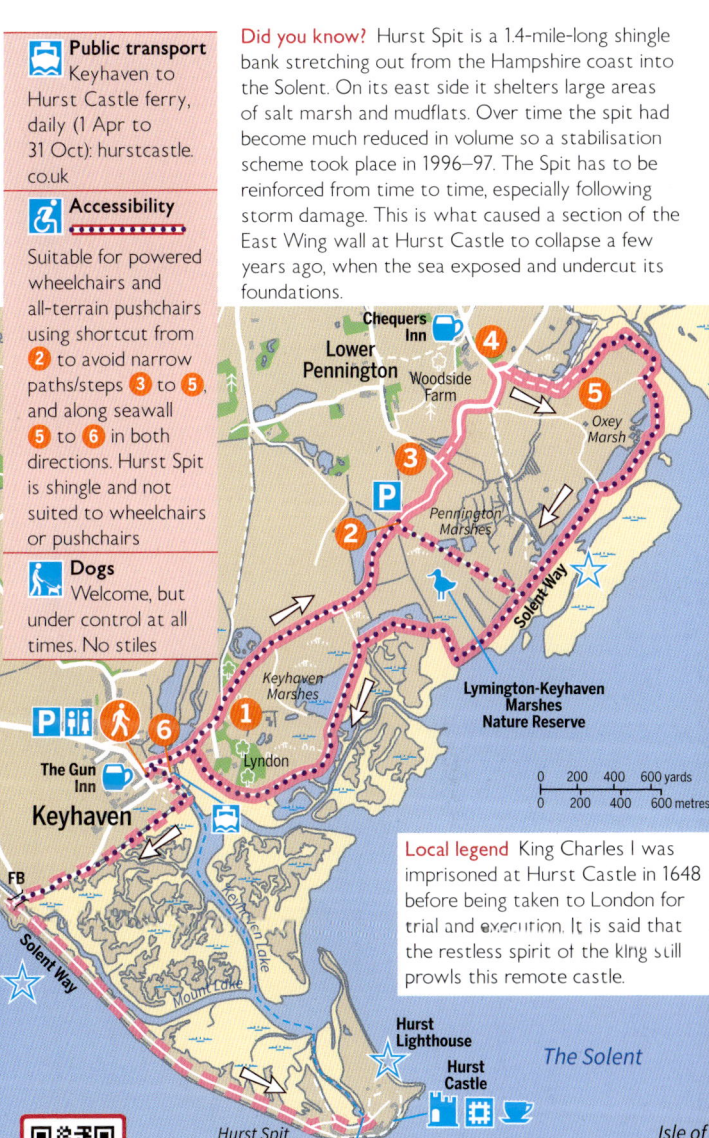

Local legend King Charles I was imprisoned at Hurst Castle in 1648 before being taken to London for trial and execution. It is said that the restless spirit of the king still prowls this remote castle.

Walk 10 Keyhaven

STORIES BEHIND THE WALK

Lymington-Keyhaven Marshes Nature Reserve Until the end of the 18th century the area from Lymington to Hurst Spit produced more sea salt than anywhere else in the country. Salt was made by impounding seawater in shallow lagoons (salterns) where it was left to evaporate. Wind pumps were then used to draw off the brine solution into large metal pans, where it was heated until only the salt remained. Lymington's fine Georgian buildings reflect the prosperity generated by salt production.

Hurst Lighthouse The first lighthouse here was built in 1786. It was followed by a second taller construction, the High Light; the original was renamed the Low Light. That was succeeded by other Low Lights and, in 1867, the High Light was replaced with a new lighthouse, which still functions today.

The Gun Inn — Road-end gate ① — ½ mile

Turn right for **Shorter loop** and to avoid narrow paths/steps — 1 mile — ②

Keyhaven car park

➤ From its entrance, head diagonally **left** across the car park to a path through a hedge gap on the far side. Turn **right** along a roadside path.

➤ Keep **forward** along the lane, cross a bridge and continue to a road-end gate.

Lymington-Keyhaven Marshes Nature Reserve

① ➤ Pass beside the gate and, ignoring a left fork in 100 yards, continue on a gravel track for over ¾ mile, along the landward side of the nature reserve, to another gate across the path.

76 Short Walks Made Easy

🏰 Hurst Castle

Situated at the end of Hurst Spit, Hurst Castle was built by Henry VIII as one of a chain of coastal fortresses to guard the Needles Passage, the narrow western entrance to the Solent. Fort Albert on the Isle of Wight is directly opposite, under a mile away. The castle was strengthened with the addition of the Victorian wing batteries; in both World Wars it was fully garrisoned. The ferry runs when the castle is open (1 Apr to 31 Oct). There are good views of The Needles (hurstcastle.co.uk).

☆ Solent Way

The waymarked Solent Way is a 60-mile long-distance path between Milford on Sea and Emsworth. As its name suggests, it runs by the Solent, but not right beside the shore all the way. Unfortunately, the New Forest's Solent coastline is largely inaccessible on foot, so at Lymington the route heads inland, initially running parallel to the coast, and thereafter following the Beaulieu River from Buckler's Hard to Beaulieu and thence via Beaulieu Heath to Hythe.

1½ miles — ③
Chequers Inn, 275 yards ahead — ④
Sluice (Moses Dock), left; steps/slope — 2 miles
⑤ Solent Way — 2½ miles

② ➡ Pass beside the gate. Beyond, walk to the far end of the parking area.
➡ **Shorter loop**: to the **right**, go through a gate. Immediately bear **left** on a gravel track heading for the coast. Ascend to the seawall and turn **right**, back to Keyhaven.
➡ **Longer loop**: keep **forward** along the lane for ¼ mile to a footpath/fingerpost (right).

③ ➡ Go **right** along the enclosed footpath.
➡ When this becomes a lane, keep **forward** along it for ¼ mile to the second signposted footpath on the right, just after a rough layby opposite.
➡ For the Chequers Inn, continue 275 yards along the lane.

NATURE NOTES

The Lymington-Keyhaven Marshes Nature Reserve encompasses coastal grassland, ponds, ditches and lagoons, with mudflats and salt marshes beyond the seawall. The varied habitats support many bird species, as well as other wildlife. Every year thousands of birds undertake extraordinary journeys to get to the Solent coast, some flying 3,000 miles from Siberia. The coastline provides an ideal place to rest and feed, mudflats offering an abundance of food. Winter visitors include Brent geese, wigeon, curlew and black-tailed godwit, all escaping from colder climes. There are also year-round residents, including oystercatcher, little egret and Canada geese.

Flowers to look out for include thrift (also known as sea pink), rock samphire, sea aster and sea campion (also found on the shingle of Hurst Spit).

In late summer, the seawall section of this walk is a good place to spot clouded yellow butterflies as they reach the mainland after their migration from Europe across the English Channel.

Oystercatcher

Solent Way

3 miles | 3½ miles

Lymington-Keyhaven

4 ▪ Turn **right** along the gravel track. In 50 yards, turn **right** by a Solent Way waymark post.
▪ Follow a gravel path beside water (left), to turn **left** through a gate in 300 yards.
▪ Keep **ahead** to steps/slope at Moses Dock (sluice).

5 ▪ Ascend the steps then keep **ahead** along the seawall path and follow the Solent Way, sea on the left, for 2¾ miles back to the road at Keyhaven.
▪ Turn **left** to retrace steps to the car park.

Publishing information

© Crown copyright 2024.
All rights reserved.

Ordnance Survey, OS, and the OS logos are registered trademarks, and OS Short Walks Made Easy is a trademark of Ordnance Survey Ltd.

© Crown copyright and database rights (2024) Ordnance Survey.

ISBN 978 0 319092 76 7
1st edition published by Ordnance Survey 2024.

ordnancesurvey.co.uk

While every care has been taken to ensure the accuracy of the route directions, the publishers cannot accept responsibility for errors or omissions, or for changes in details given. The countryside is not static: hedges and fences can be removed, stiles can be replaced by gates, field boundaries can alter, footpaths can be rerouted and changes in ownership can result in the closure or diversion of some concessionary paths. Also, paths that are easy and pleasant for walking in fine conditions may become slippery, muddy and difficult in wet weather.

If you find an inaccuracy in either the text or maps, please contact Ordnance Survey at os.uk/contact.

All rights reserved. No part of this publication may be reproduced, transmitted in any form or by any means, or stored in a retrieval system without either the prior written permission of the publisher, or in the case of reprographic reproduction a licence issued in accordance with the terms and licences issued by the CLA Ltd.

A catalogue record for this book is available from the British Library.

Milestone Publishing credits

Author: Fiona Barltrop

Series editor: Kevin Freeborn

Maps: Cosmographics

Design and Production: Patrick Dawson, Milestone Publishing

Printed in India by Replika Press Pvt. Ltd

Photography credits

Front cover: 2019 Wandering views/Shutterstock.com.
Back cover cornfield/Shutterstock.com.

All photographs supplied by the author ©Fiona Barltrop except page 6 Sue Barrett (Ordnance Survey); pages 1, 7, 27, 41 Kevin Freeborn.

The following images were supplied by Shutterstock.com: page 19 Quincy Floyd; 27 SeraphP; 39 Erni; 39 Martin Fowler; 40 CezaryKorkosz; 40 Eddie Jordan Photos; 41 ABS Natural History; 41 Dany_72; 47 2021 in_colors; 52 Sunbunny Studio; 53 Peter Kniez; 53 Rasmus Holmboe Dahl; 53 WildMedia; 59 Albert Beukhof; 59 Timbobaggins; 66 romioshots; 67 Menno Schaefer; 73 Bildagentur Zoonar GmbH; 73 ChWeiss; 73 Sandra Standbridge; 73 Stephan Morris; 79 Iva Vagnerova; 79 Lauralee Norris; 79 Rosemarie Kappler.

Top left: rock samphire
Top right: thrift
Above: clouded yellow
Left: curlew

The Gun Inn
5 miles

Ferry for Hurst Castle, left

Keyhaven car park

4 miles | 4½ miles

Marshes Nature Reserve

6 Hurst Spit

- **By boat**: after the hedge gap used to exit the car park, turn **right** to the ferry along the quayside.
- **On foot**: continue past the ferry departure point, following the seawall to join a lane.
- There's a parallel path up to the **right** as the tide can flood the lane, but either way keep **ahead** for ¼ mile to cross a footbridge and rise to the top of the shingle.
- Go **left** along the shingle ridge for 1½ miles to Hurst Castle, the lighthouse, and the ferry for the return.

Walk 10 Keyhaven